Paradoxes

Justin Leiber

Duckworth

First published in 1993 by
Gerald Duckworth & Co. Ltd.
The Old Piano Factory
48 Hoxton Square, London N1 6PB
Tel: 071 729 5986
Fax: 071 729 0015

Distributed in USA by
Focus Information Group
PO Box 369
Newburyport, MA 01950

A catalogue record for this book is available
from the British Library

ISBN 0 7156 2426 1

Typeset by Ray Davies
Printed in Great Britain by
Redwood Press Limited, Melksham

Contents

Acknowledgments

I am grateful to Professor Harris, who initiated this book and helped it on its way, to Professor William Rapaport, who gave the penultimate draft a meticulous reading, to Professor Roger Penrose for some helpful comments, and to my colleague Jim Garson for the same. Thanks are also due to my students, Keith Kaiser, Craig Larson and Mary Kay Scott, who made various contributions. I must also thank New Directions Publishing Corporation and Laurence Pollinger Ltd for permission to quote 'Borges and I' from Jorge Luis Borges's *Labyrinths*.

Introduction

This is a paradox:

This sentence is false.

It is a paradox because it dizzies and puzzles us. This book shows you that it, and its fellow conspirators, can instruct and delight us as well.

More specifically, the paradoxical sentence given above is a humble member of the notorious family of Liar paradoxes. What specifically makes this sentence paradoxical is that it has a peculiar property of instability so far as truth or falsehood go. The peculiar property is that *if it is true*, then it is false (that's what it says, it says it is false, so if it is true then it must be false), BUT *if indeed it is false*, THEN it must be true (because that is what it says, namely, that it is false). And so on, chasing its own tail endlessly, crashing its own program.

Some find it hard to believe that Liar paradoxes have spawned some of the most profound discoveries in mathematics, logic, philosophy and cognitive science. But it is so. Computer building and programming have further sharpened our sensitivity to such paradoxes. Even today computers and programs frequently go into endless loops caused by unexpected paradoxes, and there is an industry now devoted to

protecting computers and programs from malig-
nantly-designed paradoxes called *viruses*.

Chapter One gives a brief personal tour of the Liar
family's bizarre history and its future prospects in our
machines and in *us*.

Liar paradoxes aren't the only paradoxes, of course.
Some deliver a dollop of wisdom without quite the
dizziness of the Liar family. Oscar Wilde delighted in
constructing paradoxes of this sort, of which my
favourite is

Nature imitates Art.

Over two thousand years ago Aristotle made the reasonable, and even then familiar, observation that art
imitates nature. But Oscar Wilde neatly captures an
important insight. Because of the complexity of nature
we often only understand a natural process *after* we
have built an artifact that does a clearer and simpler
version of much the same job. We could not understand
how the heart and blood vessels functioned until we
built pumps, hoses and artificial circulatory systems.
Today, artificial intelligence and artificial life studies
are providing all sorts of interesting tricks for psychologists and biologists to look for in their natural
counterparts.

A related family of paradoxes concerns dream and
waking life, appearance and reality. Working up to his
famous assertion, 'I think; therefore I am', Rene Descartes delivered the paradoxical observation that
there was no way that he could tell whether the
physical world, himself included, was real or merely a
dream. In Chapter Two we take a look at the ramifi-
cations of this enthralling and frightening family of

ideas, which is as old as human culture, as profound as Shakespeare, and pops up, all by itself, in the minds of schoolchildren. To be human is to own this paradox. It comes with the territory.

Language brings the Liar family with it, consciousness brews up the appearance/reality dilemma, but we not only speak and think, we also *act*, or more specifically, we make *bets* about the future. Notoriously, and perhaps to our credit, humans are rather better at speech and consciousness than at gambling. As the circus owner P.T. Barnum is reputed to have said, 'There's a sucker born every minute'. In Chapter Three I begin with a simple gambling situation, the 'Monty Hall paradox' which schoolchildren and PhDs alike get wrong - disastrously and vehemently wrong. Besides affording you some useful protection against carnival shell games, I go on to consider two related paradoxes that are working their way through our intellectual and business culture, and even, like Oscar Wilde's paradox, telling biologists what to look for.

Since the number of paradoxes is limitless, in both our mathematical and our literary imagination, I have concentrated on three of the most central and captivating families, the ones that hit home, indeed *are home*. This means I have had to leave out many old villains and lots of devilish new ones. Hence I append a brief rogue's gallery of some of the other troublemakers.

1

The Liar Owns Up

... Let us admit the hallucinatory nature of the world. Let us seek ... unrealities which confirm that nature. We shall find them, I believe, in the antinomies of Kant and in the dialectic of Zeno. 'The greatest magician (Novalis has memorably written) would be the one who would cast over himself a spell so complete that he would take his own phantasmagorias as autonomous appearances. Would not this be our case?' I conjecture that this is so. We (the undivided divinity operating within us) have dreamt the world. We have dreamt it as firm, mysterious, visible, ubiquitous in space and durable in time; but in its architecture we have allowed tenuous and eternal crevices of unreason, which tell us it is false.

J. Borges, Labyrinths, p. 208

Paradoxically, perhaps the most available and economical, and reliable, path to immortality is this: invent a paradox. Anyone can do it, with a minimum of materials, for it may consist of but one, or a few, sentences, and it need not be written down, for its infectious intellectual structure catches us even more firmly than the verbal cues of a limerick or an advertising jingle, so that a paradox may miraculously survive intact when whispered from A to B, who whispers it to C, C in turn whispering it to D, D to E, and so on down the line to Z, the paradox's demonic replicative energy ensuring that accidental divergences in wording will not accumulate but will keep on being pulled back into a recognisable, if not improved, version such as that Z, finally, may proffer A. Even more paradoxically, the replicative energy of the paradox may conjure itself into existence, though no one in the A-Z loop may intend to create it.

The oldest known paradox is attributed in countless texts to a sixth-century BC prophet and poet of the island of Crete, Epimenides, who is reputed to have said (we have no *writings* of his, nor any firm historical record of him; even to the first historian, Herodotus, he is the stuff of fable):

All Cretans are liars.

Recalling the message passing from A to Z, other attributed versions fill the paradox out a bit, e.g.:

I am a Cretan. All Cretans are liars.

St Paul, over half a millennium later in the ramified A-Z loop, tightens the paradox up with the lawyerly addition of *always* and gnashes his teeth at the result:

One of themselves, even a prophet of their own, said, the Cretans are always liars, evil beasts, slow bellies.
This witness is true ...

Titus 1:12-13

1. *The Liar Owns Up*

St Paul's addition of *always*, like the addition of 'I am a Cretan', *does* make the paradox more explicit. There would be nothing paradoxical in a non-Cretan saying 'All Cretans are liars': it might be true or it might be false, just as is 'All swans are white' (which was once thought true but then falsified by the discovery of black swans). Similarly, there would be nothing paradoxical in 'All Cretans lie *sometimes*, particularly when money is involved' – that is the banal interpretation that St Paul's *always* explicitly rules out. But if someone says 'I, a Cretan, say that all Cretans always lie', we must realise that if what he says – *all Cretans always lie* – is true, *then* it is *false*, because this time he has told the truth, namely, that *all Cretans always lie*; HOWEVER, *since* in that case he has told the *truth*, his claim that all Cretans always lie is *false*, so he has *lied*; BUT if he has lied, then what he is saying is true, so ... ; AND SO ON (I put the *and so on* in capitals because we all know how to go on, how to keep the demon paradox rolling through the ramified A-Z loop; though called 'the Liar', the Liar is no common sneak but rather a prodigally open engine of puzzlement).

Modern, still tighter versions of the liar, eschewing quaint references to Crete, run from the self-dramatising confession

I am now lying

to the impersonal declaration

This sentence is false.

But classical or modern, the dizzying swirl is much the same. If I am now lying, my statement that I am lying

15

is true; but then, since it is true, I am not lying, so my statement is false and a lie; but, in that case ... Similarly, if this sentence is false, it speaks truly of itself, so it is true; and, contrariwise, as Tweedledum would say, if it is true, then what it says is false; and so on, and so on, endlessly.

You may have noticed that St Paul's tightening of the paradox seems merely an inadvertent concomitant of abuse. He is just piling it on. *Always*, like *evil beasts* and *slow bellies*, is just St Paul's way of ladling out abuse ('slow bellies' is the King James's bizarrely literal translation of a phrase others would put as 'lazy gluttons'). The surrounding passages, excoriating 'those of circumcision'

> Whose mouths must be stopped, who subvert whole houses, teaching things which they ought not, for filthy lucre's sake. One of themselves ... said ... This witness is true. Wherefore rebuke them sharply, that they be sound in faith, not giving heed to Jewish fables

suggest that St Paul was quite unaware that he was relaying a paradox, much less tightening it up. Paul, evidently, had heard that even some Cretan or another had preached that Cretans are liars and this opportune admission Paul embellishes with routine further abuse – evil beasts, slow bellies – figuring that any preacher who would call his fellow countryfolk liars would allow the rest naturally; all this without Paul ever noticing the completely paradoxical corner his urge to up the abuse had painted him into. For if 'this witness is true' in saying, himself one of them, that all Cretans are liars, then this Cretan witness speaks true and thus refutes the 'always lying' accusation. Indeed, St Paul is so little attentive to paradox – or simply good manners – that he fails to realise that since his letter is ostensibly addressed to Cretan Christians, his insistence that all Cretans are *always* liars belies his demand that they spread truth. This is a particularly sharp example of a paradox's demonic energy, for St Paul tightens up the paradox and sends it on, not to X or Y or Z but to billions of Bible readers, without realising what he has done and quite against his presumed preferences. Paradoxes are sneaky, free-loading on inadvertent, though perhaps not wholly undeserving, carriers.

And what is worse, paradoxes may well be self-creative. I have had my joke, painting St Paul as a savage, blockhead, puritanical doomsday preacher – which he was of course – but what slender evidence we have suggests that Epimenides himself might have been as blockhead as St Paul. If the ancients speak true, Epimenides (about the same business as the righteous Paul) was chiding Cretans for claiming that immortal Zeus was dead and his tomb in Crete by insisting that Cretans were notoriously unreliable witnesses (G. Buttrick et al., pp. 530-1). So it is quite likely that Epimenides owes his immortality to a paradox that he inadvertently issued, like an A who hisses a crude insult to B, only to find Z returning a catchy witticism.

Legend, relayed by Diogenes Laertius, has it that Epimenides lived for either 157 or 299 years (the latter figure, naturally, the Cretan position) and slept for a stretch of 57 of them, so one would like to imagine that he lived long enough to see his remark, self-transformed into the most notorious paradox in history, grinning up at him from a logic text. We cannot be sure whether to expect him to have been happy at such an intimation of immortality (St Paul, I imagine, would have snarled). While conniving at paradox may be the cheapest way to enter the artifice of eternity, you may end up wondering whether you did the job or the words themselves.

Not only history but legend repeats itself as tragedy and then as farce. Decades young but old with a history of reinventing the wheel (if not the entire history of human invention and misinvention), computer science already abounds with mythic paradoxes. In her redoubtably titled *The Devouring Fungus* (pp. 91-2) Karla Jennings relays a legend from computer science about an international conference ushering in a computer that could translate any language into English and construct a response:

The curtain rose on a glowing steel-and-glass machine the size of a refrigerator. Three visitors chosen randomly from the audience spoke to it.

'Good morning,' said a Swede in her language. 'Please estimate the number of people in this room.'

The machine paused, then replied in a soft hollow voice, 'Good morning to you. Unfortunately, such estimates are not within my power. I'm only a translator.' The crowd laughed.

An African philologist asked in Swahili, 'Do you feel peculiar, being on display?'

'Not at all,' it said. 'That is part of my function.'

Then a Turk asked, 'How are you?'

The computer shuddered as it repeated in Turkish, 'How are you? How are you? How are you?' faster and faster, until suddenly both voice and lights went dead. Four thousand people gasped.

The computer's programmer had not anticipated that the Turkish greeting 'How are you?' is literally translated as 'What is what isn't?' This simple paradox proved to be more than the computer could handle.

The (more or less) actual world probably anticipated the legend Karla Jennings relates; it certainly had plenty of preparation. Literal history records that in 1947 two Harvard undergraduates, William Burkhart and Theodore Kalin, having built the first electronic computer designed solely to solve problems in logic, asked their machine to evaluate the Liar. The machine went into oscillation, making, according to Kalin, 'a hell of a racket' (M. Gardner, p. 9). In the August 1951 issue of *Astounding Science Fiction* magazine, Gordon Dickson's 'The Monkey Wrench' has some human scientists save their lives by telling a berserk computer, 'You must reject the statement I am now making to you because all the statements I make are incorrect.'

Given that the liar paradox is the oldest and most notorious in the history of logic and mathematics, Burkhart and Kalin expected their creation to go into a fit with even more assurance than did Dickson's imagined scientists. Meeting my first electronic calculator in my early teens – a large, impressive early 1950s business machine – my first action was to button it to divide by zero. I first watched its oscillations with the Olympic amusement of the gods who set Sisyphus to an endless labour of rock rolling, though this turned to consternation when I could not stop the machine oscillations. My final, desperate move, forestalling the approach of authority, was to pull the plug. I later learned that the back of the machine had a red button one could push to abort the paradoxical operation. The newer, smaller model I ran into a few months later disappointed me in that it cunningly lacked the relevant zero button.

Obviously, one of the *first* thoughts of scientists charged to design and program a computer to be logical would be: 'Now what happens if some adolescent twerp feeds it a liar paradox?' This consideration makes Jennings's legend rather too fabulous for words. The bit about Turkish is adroitly misleading window-dressing, because the machine is supposed to get into trouble *after translating into English*. So the computer would have suffered the same breakdown if some adolescent twerp in the audience had fed it (perhaps reading out Gordon Dickson's commanding recipe) a liar paradox in English – 'as some twerp undoubtedly will' as the second thought of any early computer scientist would have been.

There can be an uneasy overtone of self-recognition in our laughter at Jennings's story. The poet Philetas of Kos reportedly grew thin and finally died, *c.* 270 BC, of brooding about the liar paradox. I recall oscillation and nausea in my first encounter with the paradox, which subsequently gave way, once I had familiarised myself with the paradox, to the adolescent amusement of infecting my schoolmates with the virus: early but judicious exposure to these cognitive viruses engenders resistance along with understanding and even wisdom. As we shall soon see, however, the endlessly-mutating liar paradox has produced some of the most profound and troubling discoveries in the entire history of human thought, troubling the most powerful minds in this century. Indeed the finale of the liar in the work of Bertrand Russell, Kurt Gödel and Alan Turing bids fair to be the most dazzling, disconcerting and foundational achievement in the history of human thought.

I wrote that Burkhart and Kalin's computer-paradoxing probably *preceded* the legend that Jennings records, but I am not sure of this. The refrigerator size of Jennings's imagined computer, its contented fawning and utter literal-mindedness (the classical owner's dream of a good slave), followed by its humanly-reassuring, complete, childish cognitive collapse, all mark Jennings's story as 1950s material, though she has not been able to pin down its origins any more than Martin Gardner (p. 76) and other paradox-mongers have been able to determine the source of the three- (or two-) pronged weapon and the crazy crate, though the weapon began circulating in the 1960s and the crate perhaps a decade earlier (see pp. 22 and 23).

There is something unsettling about stories of such recent vintage having no traceable authorship – and it is somehow still more unsettling to have such anonymous drawings, indeed objects (we have photographs of the crate as well as sketches). It reminds one of Jorge Borges's most hallucinatory work, 'Tlön, Uqbar, Orbus Tertius', in which he imagines a paradoxically-altered mirror world, described in a 40-volume transmogrification of the *Encyclopaedia Britannica*, in which idealism is common sense and belief in material objects is paradoxical nonsense, which invades our world through its stories and, finally, its paradoxical objects, which appear anonymously and spontaneously.

While, partly courtesy of St Paul, Epimenides is often credited with the Liar, Eubulides of Miletus, who

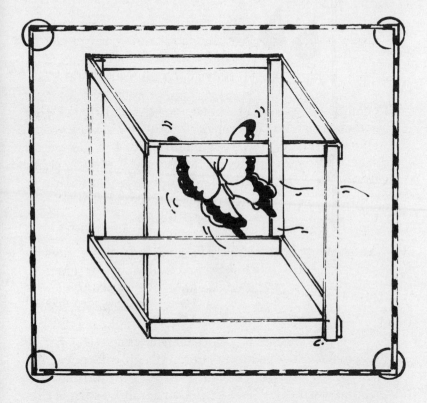

was a contemporary of Aristotle in the fourth century BC, appears to have been the first person to make a career of self-conscious and aggressive use of the paradox, giving it the tight formulation that modern versions employ:

> Does a man who says that he is now lying speak truly?
>
> Cicero, *De Divinatione* ii.11

Perhaps because Eubulides led the charge of the Megarian logicians against Aristotle and his followers, Aristotle himself makes no mention of the liar paradoxes, and so the medieval logicians apparently reinvented the Liar, in the twelfth century, in a dual version:

> Socrates says 'What Plato says is false' and Plato says 'What Socrates says is true' and neither says anything else. Is what Socrates says true or false?
>
> W. & M. Kneale, *The Development of Logic*, p. 228

This version makes it clear that you cannot get rid of the paradox by a simple ban on self-reference, by prohibiting sentences that refer to themselves through words like 'I' and 'this'. Around the turn of the century, P.E.B. Jourdain invented a more vivid and visual version of the medieval Liar. On one side of a blank card print

THE SENTENCE ON THE OTHER SIDE OF THIS CARD IS TRUE.

1. *The Liar Owns Up*

On the other side of the same card print

THE SENTENCE ON THE OTHER SIDE OF THIS CARD
IS FALSE.

Jourdain's paradox makes a nifty T-shirt. You could imagine a fourfold version in which the sentence on the front would assert true of the sentence on the right-hand side, which in turn would assert true of the sentence on the back, the back asserting the left to say true, while the left, sinisterly, would assert the front sentence to be false.

Similarly we could easily change Plato's statement to 'What Aristotle says is true' and add 'Aristotle says "What Socrates says is true"' and the paradox again appears. Indeed people can add as many more to the loop as they wish, so that no matter how many links you check out there may still lurk another that will activate the paradox.

Over the last three decades of the nineteenth century, Gottlob Frege (1848-1925) worried that paradoxes and contradictions might lurk in our understanding of the infinite fabric of the natural numbers. Frege sought to secure mathematics in a foundation of a purely logical sort, one so basic it must surely be free of paradox and contradiction. Numbers, after all, are rather peculiar things. As St Augustine observed about *time*, numbers seem to be obvious, everyday things in our world, as familiar as atoms and apple pie, as unproblematic as plants and planets, until you ask what *one, two* and *three*, or the square root of two, *really are*. What colour is *one*, and where is it, and why is there only *one* one? Ditto questions for *two, three, seven* and the smallest number that I haven't mentioned in this book.

If you check the entirety of this book to this point you will find, among the unmentioned natural numbers, a least one (*four* before I mentioned it in this very phrase) – that number, the unmentioned one, is what I am mentioning right now, of course (we both know what it has to be, so have I mentioned it?! (*five*, wasn't it – but now it is ...)). This last is a variation of what is called Berry's paradox, which specifically concerns *the smallest number that cannot be expressed in less than thirteen words*. Since the italicised expression has twelve words, to which set does the number it describes belong: the set of numbers that can be expressed with less than thirteen [English] words, or the set of numbers that can be expressed only by using more than twelve words? Either answer produces contradiction.

Kurt Grelling's paradox asks us to divide all adjectives into two sets: *self-descriptive* adjectives and *non-self-descriptive* adjectives. Adjectives such as 'polysyllabic', 'short' and 'sophisticated' are self-descriptive. Adjectives such as 'monosyllabic', 'long' and 'slang' are non-self-descriptive. Now ask yourself to which set does the adjective 'non-self-descriptive' belong?

As Jorge Borges writes of Tlön's ominous mirror objects, paradoxes come in almost self-inventing waves. Jourdain, a British mathematician, Kurt Grelling, a German one, and G.G. Berry, an Oxford University librarian, all came forth with their paradoxes at the turn of the twentieth century, in company with many other exhibitors I have not mentioned. This disturbing turn to paradox was in stark contrast to two hundred odd years of Enlightenment and progress, ushered in by Galileo and John Locke's contemptuous disdain for paradoxes as 'verbal trickery' and the poet Alexander Pope's insistence that

> ... [We turn] the tuneful art
> From sounds to things, from fancy to the heart;
> For Wit's false mirror held up Nature's light;
> Shew'd erring Pride, WHATEVER IS, IS RIGHT;
> > *An Essay on Man* IV, 390

particularly as

> Nature, and Nature's Laws lay hid in Night.
> God said, *Let Newton be!* and All was Light.
> > epitaph for Sir Isaac Newton

The word *paradox* had entered the English language with a bang, in Reformation and Elizabethan times of great intellectual uncertainty and instability. Indeed so many essays and books of the time had paradox as title or subject that Professor R.L. Colie entitled her brilliant study of the period *Paradoxica Epidemica: The Renaissance Tradition of Paradox*. Though Shakespeare, like John Donne, both mentions and uses paradoxes with considerable frequency, practically the first use recorded in the *Oxford English Dictionary* is a straightforward 1616 definition from Bullokar's chapbook:

> *Paradox*, an opinion maintained contrary to the common allowed opinion, as if one affirme that the earth doth move round and the heavens stand still.

27

Bullokar's characterisation is from the literal Greek, from which *doxa* translates as 'opinion' and *para*, more or less, as 'contrary to'. Along with Shakespeare and Donne, Bullokar also suggests that paradox is a contrary formulation that has the spice of insight and dangerous truth, as against the leaden dough of accepted opinion (by the time Alexander Pope wrote, a hundred years later, the Lord indeed had let Newton be, and be widely spread, so that the sun-centered solar system was no longer a mind-wrenching, paradoxical inversion but just enlightened common sense). After 1640, the *OED*'s paradox entries evaporate, particularly in the favourable sense; between 1698-1800 there is no entry whatsoever and through the bulk of the nineteenth century, the few entries carry the unfavourable suggestion of 'verbal trickery' or 'nonsense'. (Imagine paradoxes as gremlins, lurking in children's verbal play, in Lewis Carroll and Edward Lear, waiting to burst forth once more in the ferment of Modernity, as they had in the Renaissance. They certainly did a job on Gottlob Frege's attempt to secure the foundations of mathematics in logic.)

Frege's way to explain what the numbers *one, two, three*, etc., are is this. *One* is the set of all sets that have only one member; *two* is the set of all sets that have only two members; *three* is the set of all sets that have only three members; and so on. By a *set* he means any collection of anything, marbles, ants, paperclips, the people you met yesterday, and so on, including collections of such collections. So you could call a set with only one member a one-of-a-kind, or a *oner* (like *the first human to step on the moon* or *the largest planet in the solar system*). So Frege is saying that *one* is the set of *oners*, or *all the oners*; *two* is the set of *two-ers* (pairs); *three* is all the *three-ers* (trios); and so on.

To the natural objection, 'But you define "one" by using "*one* member",' Frege's defence lay in making the definition more explicit so that the second 'one' indeed does disappear (as follows):

One is the set of all sets such that some x is in the set and, if any y is a member, then $x = y$.

You can see how we can define 'two', 'three', and so on.

Two is the set of all sets such that x and y are in the set, x does not equal y, and if z is a member, then $z = x$ or $z = y$.

All of this may seem niggling and mindlessly long drawn out, as if the stolidly Germanic Frege were Lewis Carroll's stolidly paradoxical Duchess, who says to Alice,

'Be what you would seem to be'– or, if you'd like it put more simply – 'Never imagine yourself not to be otherwise than what it might appear to others that what you were or might have been was not otherwise than what you had been would have appeared to them to be otherwise.'

Indeed, perhaps because it appeared so simple as to be common sense to mathematicians, Frege had to produce (in his 1879 book *Begriffsschrift* [*Concept-Writing*]) the first systematic version of modern symbolic logic, simply in order to have the tools to undertake his project of reducing numbers and their qualities to logic. His various subsequent publications were stations on the way to his intended life's work, *Grundgesetze der Arithmetik* [*Fundamentals of Arithmetic*] (1902). Here numbers were to be finally grounded in firm, albeit expansive, logical foundations. An Alexander Pope of the 1900s, out of joint with the times, might have written:

> Number, and number's laws were hid in gloom
> God said *Let Frege sign and Them illume!*

In fact a darker and more impish deity was at work, and the verse of W.B. Yeats more apt:

> And what rough beast, its hour come round at last,
> Slouches towards Bethlehem to be born?

The second volume of *The Fundamentals of Arithmetic* was at the printers when Frege felt forced hurriedly to add a slender appendix that began

> A scientist can hardly encounter anything more undesirable than to have the foundation collapse just as the work is finished. I was put in this position by a letter from Mr. Bertrand Russell ...

What Russell conveyed was this. Sets divide into two sorts: sets that are *self-membering*, and sets that are *non-self-membering*. The set of oranges, for example, is not itself an orange, so the set of oranges belongs in the *non-self-membering* set; the same is true of the set of apples or of ardvaarks or of atoms, for each set is not a member of itself. On the other hand, the set of all sets is surely itself a set, so it is *self-membering*; similarly, the set of everything that is not an apple certainly is not itself an apple, so it is *self-membering*; and so on. So we have sets that are not members of themselves, and sets that are members of themselves. Russell's paradox is this: is the set of all *non-self-membering* sets a member of itself? If it is a member of itself, then it isn't, but then it is, so it isn't, so it is, isn't, is, and so on, shuttlecocking self-destructively, like Burkhard and Kalin's machine. Worse yet, once you have something that demonstrably both *is* and *isn't* in a language or logical system, it infects the whole, for by the simple rules of deduction, everything now becomes both true and false, both necessary and impossible.

Of course, it was possible to patch things up, just as we can, and do, build machines so that they don't paradox away like Burkhard and Kalin's computer or my calculator (the equivalent, for the brooding, and thinning, Philetas of Kos might be a firm injunction not to think about it, reinforced with valium). Several ways to do the patching have turned up, salving various intuitions and efficiencies, but none has commanded general satisfaction. (Frege himself offered one, but his subsequent work suggests his dissatisfaction with it or with any other response to Russell's postcard, including Russell's own response in the four volumes of *Principia Mathematica* (1910-13), with its unending hierarchy of languages in which each level can only refer to those lower than itself.)

Bertrand Russell is arguably the most significant, and certainly the most prodigal, philosopher and scientist of the last two hundred years. He was, as he most insouciantly indicates in his obituary, written thirty years before his death at the age of 97 in 1970, a person of both the nineteenth and twentieth centuries, of the confident Victorian era and of our paradoxical Modernity. Appropriately, while he laboured for two years to find a way of dealing with the set-theoretic paradoxes, he often felt that the problem was somehow trivial, that there must be a simple solution, and that he was being slightly ridiculous. Perhaps inevitably, his *Principia Mathematica* became the target for what I cannot resist calling *the revenge of the numbers*.

Principia Mathematica showed how numbers could be pictured in purely logical terms (with guards against the set paradoxes). In 1929 Kurt Gödel showed how the logical expressions, formulas and structures of *Principia* could be pictured by numbers. He then showed that *Principia*'s system contained a formula that said 'I am not provable'. The formula was true – logically and mathematically true – yet there was no way, within the system, to prove it; worse yet, if you added the formula to the axioms, new unprovables could be constructed, as many as you liked. Worst of all, you could never prove that the system as a whole was free of contradictions. As this work was generalised by Gödel and Alan Turing, what was true of *Principia* was true of any system that attempted to represent arithmetical truths. Arithmetic was incomplete and would always remain so. An even more final nightmare was in the works.

Unprovable propositions of the sort Gödel uncovered are like viruses (certainly the foreign replicators that plague today's computers are aptly named *viruses*). Is there some systematic way to identify unprovable propositions? If so, mathematicians could identify these troublemakers and wall them off from the vast world of good healthy mathematics (they could be exiled to joke books like this one, kept away from serious scientific discourse). Similarly computer scientists could then build computers with the full reach of mathematics and yet be sure that they would be safe from starting calculations that would never halt (without needing the equivalent of a red 'bail out' button). Alan Turing showed that there cannot be a way of making sure that any system of mathematics is virus-free; similarly there is no way of building a computer (that expresses mathematics) that guarantees that it won't get itself into a endless, paradoxical calculation.

Turing's proof runs as follows. The general idea is to show that a system (or a machine) for identifying unprovable propositions is impossible. First, suppose that we did have such a system (a machine) for identifying such undecidable propositions. Turing demonstrated that such a system/machine would be a variety of what we now call Universal Turing Machines, a kind of system/machine which, when fed a description of some system/machine, will turn itself into that system/machine. Turing proposed feeding this hypothetical identifier machine *its own description*. He then demonstrated that this hypothetical machine would self-destruct in paradoxical oscillations. The machine, in other words, is impossible. (As a footnote to Epimenides, who inadvertently allowed it all to begin, and to Alan Turing, who composed the grand finale, note that Epimenides' slur eventually became *upper-cased* as 'the Liar', while Alan Turing's intellectual invention, the Turing machine, became *lower-cased* by the US Library of Congress, which lists Turing's achievement as 'turing machines' and 'universal turing machines' as if Turing were not an individual human being but a force of nature, a chemical element, a geometric shape or generic mode of transportation. It is difficult to say whether Epimenides or Turing had the better of it, in the uppering and lowering. What we do know is that they epitomise paradox. One could think of worse fates.)

Turing's general result is that mathematics is thoroughly infected, with no way of surely slicing out the paradoxical stuff, nor any way of being sure that a computer we build will not unwittingly get itself into a haltless oscillation. (We can of course build in a red button or some instruction that says 'If you have spent more than a billion billion steps in a calculation, abort it'; these are stop-gaps, fail-safes, gimcracks, after-the-fact band-aids.)

In *A Shropshire Lad* A.E. Housman argues that

> ... since the world has still
> Much good, but much less good than ill,
> I'd face it as a wise man would,
> And train for ill and not for good.

Housman concludes his defence of painful and paradoxical wisdom through the metaphor of King Mithridates, who protected himself against poisoners by building up a trained immunity (rather like inoculation by systematic exposure):

> He gathered all that springs to birth
> From the many-venomed earth;
> First a little, thence to more,
> He sampled all her killing store,

1. *The Liar Owns Up*

And easy, smiling, seasoned, sound,
Sate the king when healths went round.
They put arsenic in his meat
And stared aghast to watch him eat;
They poured strychnine in his cup
And shook to see him drink it up:
They shook, they stared as white's their shirt:
Them it was their poison hurt.
– I tell the tale that I heard told.
Mithridates, he died old.

This would do well as the motto for any course of paradoxes. They are also fun, as is Housman's poem. And we now know, courtesy of Alan Turing, what we already suspected, that we will never run out of paradoxes, nor be proof against startlement.

(Mithridates was Late Republican Rome's most crafty and proteanly dangerous eastern opponent. He indeed so classically exemplified self-inoculation that he is lower-cased in dictionaries. Mithridates was mithridative – and paradoxical to boot. When, in his seventies, he was finally trapped, the tale is that he was unable to kill himself with a course of poisons, so successful had he been at self-inoculation, and hence he had to run on a sword. The reader should be warned that the ancients and certainly Housman were capable of wishful exaggeration. While one can build up tolerance to many poisons – nicotine, barbiturate and even strychnine, to mention a few – arsenic accumulates in the body over time and so small doses over time can become lethal.)

If we think that the point of education and research, of our whole cognitive existence, is the accumulation of truths, like stocking the shelves of a library, we are likely to misunderstand paradoxes. Biologist Richard Dawkins, in *The Selfish Gene*, gives us the path to understanding the force and status of paradoxes, both through his revisionary conception of genes as selfish and through his coinage of the term *memes* to label the citizens of our cognitive life, replicators which Dawkins shows us have many features corresponding to genes.

It is of course paradoxical to say that genes – substrings of DNA – are *selfish*, as if one imagines a group of quarrelsome and competitive individuals, plotting and planning against each other. The traditional view is that biological evolution consists of the competition of various organisms, or kinds of organisms, against each other. The idea that the species is the competitor, that it is the selfish species, runs into a roadblock: members of species often compete with each other and are rarely anything like altruistic; moreover there is no collective planning mechanism (no central party committee) to explain the source of pan-special activity. On the other hand, if we think that the 'selfish' individual organism is the ultimate competitor, we run into the obvious point that much individual organism behaviour is obviously self-destructive, particularly behaviour that serves to preserve the individual's genes at the cost of the future of the individual organism (think of the salmon self-mutilating and self-destructing as it struggles up narrow freshwater streams to deposit its eggs and die, of the many insects for whom sexual intercourse is eagerly-sought sure suicide, of the extraordinary risks most animals will run to reproduce or protect progeny). Dawkins points out that the only replicators that have a chance of immortality, that sit at the centre of the mechanical process of replication, are the genes themselves: they bear their selfishness on their mechanical sleeve – their self-replication is their very being – and organisms such as ourselves are their survival machines, their unwitting but effective way of realising their chance of immortality.

Enter the *meme*, the new replicator, that reproduces itself, nesting virally, in the linguistic, perceptual, and cognitive apparatus of the human gene survival machine. The Liar, and the other paradoxes, are perhaps the most honest of these memic replicators, for the Liar (like the other paradoxes) shows its replicative structure openly and instructively: if you are being conned or merely co-opted, you are certainly given every chance to see it. The Liar is no liar.

The shift in our viewpoint represented by the coinage of *meme* is well put in philosopher Daniel Dennett's wonderful line,

> A scholar is just a library's way of making another library.
>
> D. Dennett, *Consciousness Explained*, p. 202

And where do we stand, survival host machines for both genes and memes as we are? Dennett reflects:

> I don't know about you, but I am not initially attracted by the idea of my brain as a sort of dung-heap in which the larvae of other people's ideas reproduce themselves, before sending out copies of themselves in an informational Diaspora. It seems to rob my mind of its importance as an author and a critic. Who is in charge, according to this vision – we or our memes?

There is, of course, no simple answer. We would like to think of ourselves as godlike creators of ideas, manipulating them as our whim dictates, judging them all from an independent, Olympian standpoint. But even if this is our ideal, we know that it is seldom if ever the reality, even with the most masterful and creative minds. As Mozart allegedly observed of his own brainchildren:

When I feel well and in a good humour, or when I am taking a drive or walking after a good meal, or in the night when I cannot sleep, thoughts crowd into my mind as easily as you would wish. Whence and how do they come? I do not know and *I have nothing to do with it*.

Of course, as Dennett would be the first to admit, we have the same dilemma from the gene end. In effect, we want to think that we are the creators of our own genes (or rather creators of the causal effects of these genes in our behaviour), and it is unsettling to think that what we do is (when not memic) the product of the pushes and pulls of our selfish genes, exercising themselves against the environment in their survival quest.

But perhaps the poet Jorge Borges gives us the most vivid representation of the tension between genetic and memetic viewpoints. He displays this tension, memicises it, in an extended paradox, one that is pure meme and, at the same time, an instructive picture of the interplay between meme and gene, mind and body, subjectivity and objectivity. His text will also serve as a bridge to our next chapter.

1. The Liar Owns Up

The other one, the one called Borges, is the one things happen to. I walk through the streets of Buenos Aires and stop for a moment, perhaps mechanically now, to look at the arch of an entrance hall and the grillwork on a gate; I know of Borges from the mail and see his name on a list of professors or in a biographical dictionary. I like hourglasses, maps, eighteenth-century typography, the taste of coffee and the prose of Stevenson; he shares these preferences, but in a vain way that turns them into the attributes of an actor. It would be an exaggeration to say that ours is a hostile relationship; I live, let myself go on living, so that Borges may contrive his literature, and this literature justifies me. It is no effort for me to confess that he has achieved some valid pages, but those pages cannot save me, perhaps because what is good belongs to no one, not even to him, but rather to the language and to tradition. Besides, I am destined to perish, definitively, and only some instant of myself can survive in him. Little by little, I am giving over everything to him, though I am aware of his perverse custom of falsifying and magnifying things. Spinoza knew that all things long to persist in their being; the stone eternally wants to be a stone and the tiger a tiger. I shall remain in Borges, not in myself (if it is true that I am someone), but I recognise myself less in his books than in many others or in the laborious strumming of a guitar. Years ago I tried to free myself from him and went from the mythologies of the suburbs to the games with time and infinity, but those games belong to Borges now and I shall have to imagine other things. Thus my life is a flight and I lose everything and everything belongs to oblivion, or to him.

I do not know which of us has written this page.

Labyrinths, p. 246

Paradox memes are unmaskers, teachers, that show us, like the pun more generally and banally, the blinkered insecurity of our thought. Borges is playful and paradoxical, a mastermemer who is memorably mithridative.

2

The Dreamer Wakes

One night I dreamed I was a butterfly, fluttering
hither and thither, content with my lot. Suddenly
I awoke and I was Chuang-tzu again. Who am I
in reality? A butterfly dreaming that I am
Chuang-tzu or Chuang-tzu imagining he was a
butterfly?

S. Brook, *The Oxford Book of Dreams,* p. 256

Appropriate to its first-person frame, it is not the
existence of the 'I' that is in question, but rather its
nature, butterfly or man. Indeed, as the passage con-
tinues, the author adds that Chuang-tzu and the butterfly share the state of becoming as against being. In
being, one presumes, the 'I' and identifiable will would
be lost in the disappearance of mind into seamless
nature. In *Through the Looking Glass* Lewis Carroll
gives us a more divisive, third-person version of
Chuang-tzu's paradox.

Alice, who had slept to dream her pell-mell entry to
Wonderland when she followed the White Rabbit
through a hole in the ground, now dreams a more
paradoxical entry to unreality through the mirror over
her fireplace, an entry in which matters become
stranger and stranger as she leaves the part of the
looking-glass world visible in it. Looking-glass-world
Tweedledum tells Alice that she exists only in the

looking-glass Red King's dream of her and that, should the King awake, Alice will disappear. Of course, since the Red King exists only in Alice's dream, he will disappear should she awaken. The situation is most satisfyingly paradoxical if we take Alice and the Red King to be symmetrical so far as existence goes: that if *either* wakes up, the other and his or her world disappears, taking the looking-glass world to be as real as this one. The version in which Alice is the real dreamer, and the Red King and his dream only parts of her dream, is much less unsettling, indeed prosaic. To someone who points out that, after all, Alice is real and she is dreaming the Red King, we may happily reply that *she is nothing but a character in a book*, a narrative word dream of Lewis Carroll.

Happier still (shades of 'Borges and I'), Lewis Carroll is the pen name, the narrative persona and dream invention, of Charles Dodgson, lifelong Student (fellow) of Christ Church, Oxford, and with all but beautiful young girls, the very model of stammering reserve and hypercritical punctiliousness, who always walked 'as if he had swallowed a poker' and who specified that all letters sent to 'L. Carroll, Christ Church', should be returned 'addressee not known'. Was Lewis Carroll the affectation, the covert act, of legal citizen Charles Dodgson, or was Charles Dodgson the dissimulation, the mask, the protective disguise, of girl-child lover (and nude nymph photographer) Lewis Carroll? (Charles Dodgson's invariable response to questions about 'L. Carroll' was the bleakly past-tensed, third person, 'Mr Dodgson neither claimed nor acknowledged any connection with the books not published under his name.') This calls to mind (mine and soon yours) another Borges creation, 'Everything and Nothing,' which describes a man who had no one inside, only words. He flees from nothingness to London and the profession of actor and playwright, in which he dreams himself as many people, only eventually to retire to Stratford to become 'a retired impresario, concerned with loans, law suits, and petty usury'; at death he tells how he yearned to be one unified self, to which God's response is

'Neither am I anyone; I have dreamt the world as you dreamt your work, my Shakespeare, and among the forms in my dream are you, who like myself are many and no one.'

Labyrinths, p. 249

Shakespeare wrote in zenith days of paradox. The inversions of dream and reality, words and things, flow effortlessly in even his best known sonnet:

Shall I compare thee to a summer's day?
Thou art more lovely and more temperate:
Rough winds do shake the darling buds of May,
And summer's lease hath all too short a date:
Sometime too hot the eye of heaven shines,
And often is his gold complexion dimm'd;
And every fair from fair sometime declines,
By chance, or nature's changing course, untrimm'd;
But thy eternal summer shall not fade,
Nor lose possession of that fair thou owest;
Nor shall Death brag thou wander'st in his shade,
When in eternal lines to time thou growest;
  So long as men can breathe, or eyes can see,
  So long lives this, and this gives life to thee.

2. The Dreamer Wakes

While Shakespeare openly celebrates the reality of words against things, stage against reality, Liu Changqing (709-780), in 'Seeking the Taoist Priest Chang Shan's Retreat at South Stream,' with less obvious arrogance, apparently spins the other way,

> All along the way, where I've passed,
> The moss reveals sandals' traces.
> White clouds cling to the quiet isles;
> Fragrant grass shuts the unused gate.
> After Rain, I view the pines' colour;
> Following the mountain, I reach the water's source.
> Riverside flowers and Chan's meaning
> Face to face, also forgetting words.
>
> J. Liu, *Language – Paradox – Poetics*, p. 61

Perhaps the most fundamental theme of Chinese poetry (and Plato) is the emptiness, the futility, the irrelevance, the inevitable falseness of words, though always with this unspoken and thereby spoken caveat: *but this truth is comprised, like Shakespeare's, of words*. In 1921 Ludwig Wittgenstein published an entire book, the *Tractatus Logico-Philosophicus*, whose conclusion is that all its sentences are meaningless, a ladder that the reader must climb to command a clear view of the world and the nonexistence of the ladder (his notion that words have meaning only as transparent pointers to objects echoes Changqing's 'Face to face, also forgetting words'). In his later work, critical of the whole *Tractatus* viewpoint, Wittgenstein claimed that his aim was analogous to that of teaching a fly how to get out of an inverted glass bottle in which it would persistently buzz about the upward portion toward the light, rather than exiting downward through the bottle's opening. Against the intoxicating light of the metaphysical 'I', the arrogance of consciousness, *endarkenment* is what is needed, for then the fly will fall down and out of the bottle.

While the beloved that Shakespeare addresses has long been absorbed, paradoxically and wholly, into Shakespeare's living syllables, Alice still is not wholly Lewis Carroll's words. Alice Pleasance Liddell, the ten-year-old to whom Charles Dodgson first narrated *Alice's Adventures Underground* and who relentlessly pestered him into writing it down and publishing it as *Alice in Wonderland*, is present in one of two nineteenth-century photographs thought worthy of that notable 500 picture photographic collection of human visages, Steichen's *The Family of Man* (photographer, Charles Dodgson, 1862). Her ten-year-old face is perfect: confident, elfin, beautiful beyond belief. Her face in her twenties, in Julia Margaret Cameron's 1873 photograph, is wrenchingly handsome, ardently wise. Their last, and unrecorded, meeting was in his Christ Church rooms, her sister Rhoda discreetly ensconced nearby, Mrs Hargeaves and C. L. Dodgson congenial but hardly concupiscent (did he stammer?), hovered over by Alice and Lewis, the words that were their past, and their only future.

René Descartes (1596-1660), on the cusp of the transition from *paradoxica epidemica* to the paradox-disparaging Enlightenment, bedazzled three hundred years of European thought with a rendition of the dream paradox so timely and powerful, and so knit with the success and threat of modern science, that it swept all before it, coming to seem not paradox but the very foundation, the forge of truth and reality, the touchstone of reason. In his first meditation, while

2. *The Dreamer Wakes*

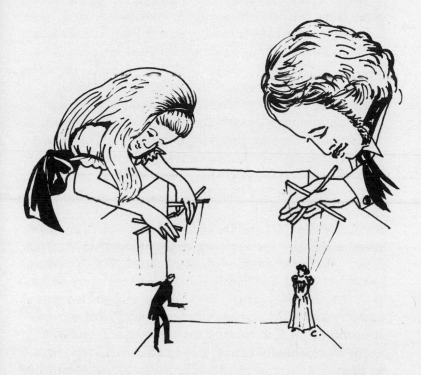

reflecting that his senses may mislead him about tiny or distant objects, he finds it impossible to doubt that he is 'in this place, seated by the fire, clothed in a dressing gown' and 'that I hold in my hands this piece of paper'. Indeed Descartes recognised (though not those who latterly practised 'Cartesian doubt') how very paradoxical his new suggestion would be, that is, to doubt such obvious facts would be to be

> classed with persons in a state of insanity, whose brains are so disordered by dark bilious vapors as to make them assert that they are monarchs when they are in greatest poverty, or clothed in purple when destitute of covering, or that their head is made of clay, their body of glass or that they are gourds? I should be as insane as they...

None the less Descartes reflects that he has often dreamt that he was sitting dressed, and writing on paper, while he slept undressed abed. There are no immediate and absolutely conclusive marks by which to distinguish sleeping from waking, and so Descartes reasons that 'I almost persuade myself that I am now dreaming' and that having thoughts is not equivalent to having a wakeful brain. Though Descartes now goes on to evoke the possibility of a malignant demon who may mislead him about all but the bare existence of his own consciousness, he is well aware of the madly paradoxical character of his argument, and he eventually concludes that he has a right, through his reason and his senses, to a cautious belief in an external physical world replete with dressing-gowns, hands, papers, etc., and indeed to some level of assurance that he is specifically supplied with these and, further, is awake. He takes it as absolutely obvious that physical brain events occasion many mental experiences and vice versa. Above all, Descartes wants to shave off the vagaries of sensory input from the mind's natively developed power to think spatially and arithmetically and to command the infinity of structures expressible in words.

The subsequent tradition, however, eagerly and confidently bought his assertion of the reality and independence of mental experience, and held that the world of mechanism, of physical objects interacting in accord with physical laws, was a dream, a mythology invented by naive materialists, who ignorantly supposed that things could exist apart from mental experience of them, apart from their appearance in the dream worlds of minds. As the theist Bishop Berkeley put it, as well as the agnostic David Hume, the world cannot be anything apart from our experience of it. To be perceived, which is indistinguishable from being dreamed, is to be. Any existence, apart from this dream sort, is inconceivable.

Respecting this tradition, Sigmund Freud observed that philosophy is what paranoia caricatures, as religion is caricatured by the rituals of compulsion neurosis, for the paranoid, with implausible egotism, argues that there is a conspiracy to delude him (or her), while Berkeley and Hume argue for an illusion so necessarily universal and common to us all that it is the very stuff of reality, universally likely to give rise to the incoherent delusion that there is a physical world of non-mental objects, a world apart from our dreams. Hence, even early in this century, Bertrand Russell, along with a horde of philosophers and scientists, continued confidently to assert that psychology was the fundamental science, since the world of physical objects described by physics was its dream. Jorge Borges clearly intended his world of Tlön, in which enduring physical objects are an inconceivable joke, as the dreamt world that Berkeley, Hume and Russell insisted was the only conceivable reality.

Only explicit paradoxers could understand such an inversion as a paranoid nightmare, rather than an avowed professional rite of thought that smoothly dominated philosophical and scientific discourse for the 250 years between Descartes and Borges. Descartes, indeed, chose his career as a result of three *real* dreams he had the night of 10 November 1618. The first two were abrupt nightmares, the second of which woke him to a room momentarily strewn with 'fiery sparks', for which Descartes found a physiological explanation. The prolonged dream Descartes found to be an allegory which he proceeded to interpret, while still asleep, as the demand that he dedicate himself to a unified science of physics, physiology and mathematics. The anti-materialist, sceptical empiricists who followed in his wake did not take the dreams of sleep seriously, having made the waking world a dream.

Recent work on dreams confirms Descartes's physiological perspective. In dreamless sleep our eyes and brain waves behave quite differently from when we are awake. When we dream, however, our brain waves shift to much like waking mode and our eyes engage in the same very rapid, criss-cross scanning movements that characterise our visual activity while awake. Indeed in dream sleep the motion and colour receptors on the retina begin to fire off neurologically as they do when light strikes them in wide-awake 'lids open' seeing. In waking vision, our brain constructs and fills in an experience of a three-dimensional world of moving objects from some fairly meagre two-dimensional retinal input (rapid eye movements are a necessary part of this process). So it seems likely that what we *see* in our dreams are visual construals initiated and fuelled by coincidences in random retinal firings, which are given, and manipulated by, narrative interpretation and even plenty of the beginnings of co-ordinated motor responses, though of these all but those that fire off the eye movements are (fortunately) almost entirely inhibited from getting to our muscles. Having the same neurological system serve as camera and projector, receiver and creator (hearer and speaker) is a typical economy of nature; computer hardware and software engineers have found themselves driven to similar economies.

(Descartes's dream meme is perennially infective. My daughter Casey first wondered out loud whether she was awake or dreaming while standing in our bathtub and looking at her face in the mirror. She was five years old. Now seven, she recently, again looking in the mirror from the tub, reverted to the issue, speculating that one test might be to 'do something silly like stick your finger in your eye, or something, and see if people did something like you were strange'. In our conversation Casey preserved the sure, cheery sense that we were talking to each other about a delightfully perplexing conundrum, while all the while allowing that we might both be imaginary partners to her dream. From the age of three Casey has used the eighteenth-century contraction, *amn't*, as in 'I'm going, amn't I', with the sure confidence of someone who knows that this is (which it is) a natural part of the English language, though she has never heard others speak so. She gives the same natural assurance to her engagement with the dream paradox.)

In this century we have awakened to rediscover the physical world, including organisms like ourselves with brains, whose properties, when described by analogy with software at the 'wetware' level, comprise mind and consciousness. Most strange indeed, we cognitive machines have awakened to discover that our consciousness is, in telling respects, often a kind of dream, a just so story, of ourselves – a plausible illustrated narration that runs along rationalising and *making sense of* the activity of our enormously complex, and mostly unconscious, cognitive apparatus, much as we do in comprehending other humans. The point is not only that, as Dennett suggests, our brain is a dung-heap in which the larvae of other people's ideas reproduce themselves. Further, our conscious awareness is often more a public relations spokesperson or cheerleader for the various specialists – the faculties – operating below or beyond consciousness. Still, it is us, the only personhood we have, our awakened dream, perhaps most genuinely displayed in sleep, in reverie, in imagination, when the happenstance, sensory pressure of the world has least purchase on us. That lover of nature and scorner of convention and fashion, Henry David Thoreau, puts it best:

Dreams are the touchstones of our characters. We are scarcely less afflicted when we remember some unworthiness in our conduct in a dream, than if it had been actual, and the intensity of our grief, which is our atonement, measures the degree by which this is separated from an actual unworthiness. For in dreams we but act a part which must have been learned and rehearsed in our waking hours, and no doubt could discover some waking consent thereto. If this meanness had not its foundation in us, why are we grieved at it? In dreams we see ourselves naked and acting out our real characters, even more clearly than we see others awake. But an unwavering and commanding virtue would compel even its most fantastic and faintest dreams to respect its ever-wakeful authority; as we are accustomed to say carelessly, we should never have *dreamed* of such a thing. Our truest life is when we are in dreams awake.

> H.D. Thoreau, *A Week on the Concord and Merrimack Rivers*, 1849

3

The Gambler's Choice

God does not play dice with the universe.

Albert Einstein

Something surprising, a paradox, is a paradox only in a particular, as it were defective, surrounding. One needs to complete this surrounding in such a way that what looks like a paradox no longer seems one.

Wittgenstein, *Remarks on the Foundations of Mathematics*, para 410

From 1963 to 1990, Monty Hall compèred 4,500 performances of 'Let's Make a Deal', a TV show in which contestants were asked to choose one of three doors. Behind one door was an expensive car, behind the other two stuff of comparatively little value (call them goats). The reader's imagination is invited to supply the pop music, the audience applause and screams, the gambling contestants' tension and tears of triumph and defeat, Monty Hall's confidently tricky manner (Mephistopheles in golf course mufti), and the madcap La-La land of Hollywood romantic hypermaterialism. After the contestant selected a door, Monty Hall would often open one of the other doors, to show a goat, while leaving two doors unopened. Hall would then offer the contestant the possibility of changing from one unopened door to the other. Frequently he would offer the contestant money to change or not change doors. He did not lose many cars.

He also inadvertently fathered a discussion of the 'Monty Hall Paradox' among mathematicians that raged in the popular press for nearly a year, culminating in a front-page article in the *Sunday New York Times* on 21 July 1991.

In a September 1990 issue of possibly the most widely distributed US Sunday supplement magazine, *Parade,* Marilyn vos Savant initiated the debate in her column 'Ask Marilyn'. (To someone who might wonder why ask Marilyn in particular, her weekly column specifies that Ms vos Savant is listed in the *Guinness Book of World Records* Hall of Fame for 'Highest IQ', viz., 228.) As she first put the puzzle,

> Suppose you're on a game show, and you're given the choice of three doors: Behind one door is a car; behind the others, goats. You pick a door, say No. 1, and the host, who knows what's behind the other doors, opens another door, say No. 3, which has a goat. He then says to you, 'Do you want to pick door No. 2?' Is it to your advantage to take the switch?

Ms vos Savant's answer was 'Yes, you should switch'.

Since vos Savant gave this answer, she has received some 10,000 letters in response, the great majority in disagreement with her. Some 1,000 of the letters came from PhDs, and indeed her most vehement critics have been mathematicians and scientists, who exulted in vos Savant's supposed error and deplored the national innumeracy that it exhibited. Robert Sachs, mathe-

matics professor at George Mason University, gave the prevailing view that there was no reason to switch doors:

> You blew it! Let me explain: If one door is shown to be a loser, that information changes the probability of either remaining choice – *neither of which has any reason to be more likely* – to 1/2. As a professional mathematician, I am very concerned with the general public's lack of mathematical skills. Please help by confessing your error and, in the future, being more careful.

Even after vos Savant wrote several columns in defence of her position, E. Ray Bobo, mathematics professor at Georgetown University, insisted, 'You are utterly incorrect.' He, too, plaintively worried about

> the national crisis in mathematical education. How many irate mathematicians are needed to get you to change your mind?

Actually by that time the mathematicians were beginning to come to her defence, along with the several thousand school-children that vos Savant got to test out the puzzle in action, who found over hundreds of trials that however one reasoned about it, you did twice as well if you shifted doors. Even the redoubtable Dr. Sachs eventually, and handsomely, wrote her that 'after removing my foot from my mouth, I'm now eating humble pie'.

It helps to think of the puzzle as follows. Initially, when you choose among the three doors, it is obvious, and all agree, that you have a one in three chance of picking the car. (Similarly, if there were at the start only two doors, one with a car and the other with a goat, your chances would be one in two.) Another way to put this is to say that when you choose one of three, two-thirds of the time you will be wrong. Now since the master of ceremonies knows which doors the goats are behind, he will *always* be able to open a door with a goat behind it after your first choice; since two-thirds of the time the car will be behind one of his two doors, he doesn't change the odds by opening one of them. Therefore you double your chances from 1/3 to 2/3 by switching doors. This was also the result obtained when Monty Hall ran the puzzle through twenty trials on his dining-room table on Thursday, 18 July 1991.

You can review the same point from another direction if you consider a shell game con. Imagine a gambler, call him Fast Eddie, who presents you with an array of three walnut shells, beneath one of which there is a pea. You pick one of the shells. The gambler (or swindler) offers you an even-money bet – if you've picked the shell with the pea, you win, say, $10, and if you haven't you lose $10. You protest that that is not a fair bet because your chance of having picked the right shell is only one in three. Fast Eddie says, 'Now I tell you what I'm going to do, I'll even the odds.' He proceeds to turn over one of the other shells, which has no pea, saying, 'Now it is fifty/fifty, so the bet is fair!' But you can see that the bet is not fair, for your one in three chance has not changed.

Having recognised this, one's natural inclination is to say to the gambler, 'Since the bet is even, like you say, why not let me change my bet to the other shell.' One reasons, correctly, that this will double one's chances (it is just the Monty Hall paradox all over again). And this may lead one to think that Fast Eddie will have to save face, and likely lose money, by letting one switch; either that, or he will, with a red face, admit that one has caught him out. This is all very well in theory, but if one is facing a professional con man, a swindler in a carnival or on a street corner, it is a mistake to proceed so, for he is an experienced professional, and you his mark. Through sleight of hand or some other means he will win.

In all such cases it is as well to recall the fatherly advice attributed to W.C. Fields:

> Son, sometime in your life, you will go into a saloon where there will be a man at the bar who will put a deck of cards on the counter and offer to bet you that he can, without touching it, make the jack of diamonds leap out of the pack and spit vinegar in your ear.
>
> Son, you must not take that bet, for otherwise you will surely end with an earful of vinegar.

While it is true that vos Savant is absolutely right, given the straightforward interpretation of her formulation of the problem, the brevity with which she originally expressed it gives the sharpster some wriggle room. If you reread her formulation, you can see that, for the sake of brevity, she does not perhaps make it fully explicit that the game show host is required on every occasion, after the contestant has made a first choice, to open a goat-backed door, then to offer the change of doors, and to do nothing else to affect the contestant's choice.

After the twenty trials that precisely bore out vos Savant's views, Monty Hall could not resist reverting to the real tactics of 'Let's Make a Deal', and then some. He suggested ten more trials.

On the first, the contestant picked Door 1.

'That's too bad,' Mr Hall said, opening Door 1. 'You've won a goat.'

'But you didn't open another door yet or give me a chance to switch.'

'Where does it say that I have to let you switch every time? I'm the master of the show. Here, try it again.'

On the second trial, the contestant again picked Door 1. Mr Hall opened Door 3, revealing a goat. The contestant was about to switch to Door 2 when Mr Hall pulled out a roll of bills.

'You're sure you want Door No. 2?' he asked. 'Before I show you what's behind that door, I will give you $3,000 in cash not to switch to it.'

'I'll switch to it.'

'Three thousand dollars,' Mr Hall repeated, shifting into his famous cadence. 'Cash. Cash money. It could be a car, but it could be a goat. Four thousand.'

'I'll try the door.'

'Forty-five hundred. Forty-seven. Forty-eight. My last offer: Five thousand dollars.'

'Let's open the door.'

'You just ended up with a goat,' he said, opening the door.

New York Times, Sunday, 21 July 1991

Monty Hall proceeded to win all ten trials by this forceful con. Every time someone picked a goat on their first pick (two-thirds of the time), he nailed them by immediately opening their door – which of course violated vos Savant's formulation, but the Monty Hall who hosted 4,500 Deal shows simply faced down the contestants in his dining room. When they initially picked the car, he conned them into switching their choice by his apparent overwhelming eagerness to get them to agree not to switch (and so they ended with several earfuls of vinegar). Under *this* Monty Hall regimen, switching is not only no longer likely to win two-thirds of the time: it will never win.

One moral of this story is that humans are not at all good at reasoning about probabilities. A much more irrational, but more general, even proverbial and pervasive mistake is dubbed the gambler's fallacy. Suppose you are tossing a perfectly ordinary six-sided die. You happen to throw a two four times in a row. Are your chances of rolling two the next time around the usual one in six? – Aren't the odds supposed to right themselves? – Doesn't a long run of red on the roulette wheel mean that black is a good bet – Isn't a new shell hole just the place to hide through an artillary barrage because another shell surely won't drop in the same place?

Consider the shell hole case. Imagine our stretch of battlefield cut into, say, ten thousand hexagons (as they do in board-game simulations). Roughly, a shell takes out a hexagon. If shells land at random, then our chances are 10,000 to one that a particular shell will hit our hex, call it 83/47. The first shell in the series arrives, blasting hex 23/27. What now are the chances that the next shell will hit 23/27? Under our assumption of randomness the answer is 10,000 to one, which is just the same as its chance of hitting any other hex, including ours. Of course the chance of *two shells in a row* hitting a particular hex, say our 83/47, is one in 10,000 times one in 10,000, or one in 100,000,000. Once, however, the first shell has landed – a one in 10,000 shot – then all you need is another one in 10,000 shot to get the two in a row result. The upshot is that it makes no sense to shift from our 83/47 to the shell-shocked 23/27.

Much the same follows for roulette and dice. A die is a cube with one, two, three, four, five and six dots on its respective sides. If it is a true, or properly constructed, die, the chances of any particular number of dots coming up is one in six, so after you happen to throw four twos in a row, the chance of a two next time is the same as always, namely, one in six. Similarly a fair, or properly constructed, roulette wheel alternates red and black slots, each of which provides an equally likely resting place for the ball, so after a long run of red, the chances still remain even that the next will be black.

Given our assumption of randomness in shelling, there not only is no advantage to moving to cratered hex 83/47, there is no disadvantage, either. Is our assumption of randomness reasonable? Strictly speaking there are no wholly random events in our world except at the subatomic level (which is why measures of time are now based on rates of radioactive decay). What some battlefields, roulette wheels and dice provide is an approximation of randomness, one that, given our measuring instruments, amounts to randomness *for our practical purposes*. Hence we vacillate between an objective and a subjective view about probabilities: we attribute the randomness to the law-like physical properties of the world or to our sense of what an ideally competent human gambler would bet.

In the case of battlefields we may find that, over some stretch of our territory, shells seem in fact to be arriving randomly, *or* we may judge this to be likely because of what we know about the accuracy of the enemy's equipment and about the area he will plan to strike. But perhaps shell blast 83/47 is the first of a series to be fired from a single, extremely accurate gun, whose instructions are either: (1) fire your next shot at another range and direction setting; *or* (2) fire your next shot with exactly the same range and direction setting. If the first case obtains, then 83/47 is prime real estate, the safest place in the battlefield; if the second, it is by far the most dangerous.

The *raison d'être* of roulette wheels and dice, as opposed to battlefields, is randomness. That is why we talk of a *true*, properly-constructed, die, or a *fair*, properly-constructed, roulette wheel. Hence, if a die rolls two four times in a row, it is usually appropriate to continue to presume its *truth*, and that being so, the chances of a two next time remain one in six. However, it is easy to imagine contexts in which you would do well to forestall an earful of vinegar. Suppose that Fast Eddie, who has sipped one beer and is acting like he has had six and is dumb happy indeed, has dropped a die four times and got two each time. He says to Slumming Sebastian, the millionaire who is more than comfortable, beer and buddy wise, 'Four times I rolled two, do you believe that! You know it can't go on, the odds got to right themselves, must be a hundred to one that it won't be another two next time, why that would be *five twos in a row*, why you couldn't do that hardly ever!' (*If* the dice are true, the chances of rolling five twos in a row are one in 7,746; none the less, given that you have happened to throw four twos in a row, the chances that the next will be a two remain, of course, one in six.)

Our scenario affords us two denouements, depending on how Slumming Sebastian rises to the bait. (1) Suppose Slumming Sebastian, knowing about 'the gambler's fallacy', replies that it is not all that unlikely, and (thinking himself sly) adds that maybe it is just a twenty or thirty to one shot. Fast Eddie will protest that it would be taking candy from a baby to accept such a bet. Then he will allow himself to be argued into the bet (with Slumming Sebastian thinking that it is he who is extracting the candy). Finally, money on the table, Fast Eddie will roll something other than a two and pocket the proceeds (and possibly the die). (2) Suppose Slumming Sebastian, quite in thrall to the gambler's fallacy, agrees that another roll of two is improbable (indeed, he slyly thinks, even more improbable than Eddie thinks). Now Eddie, slurring and lopsidedly smiling, will audibly argue himself into the view that while Sebastian is totally right, it just might be that some mysterious force is giving him the twos. Again feeling that the bet is too good to be true, Sebastian puts down five to one that Eddie won't get another two. Sebastian will now learn that the bet, indeed, is too good to be true (like the die, which will roll two any time Eddie wants it to), and again Eddie will pocket the money and the evidence.

Corresponding to the 'gambler's fallacy' is what might be called the 'it can't be a coincidence!' fallacy. This family of fallacies ranges from our tendency to forget that even the most improbable configurations become probable, even close to certain, in the long run (if not the short as well), our tendency to interpret any such supposed trend as malignant or benign attention to us, in particular, and our tendency to ignore countervailing incidents. For example, Nervous Nightingale may feel moments of nervous, imagined crash death about her son Bob every time he takes an airflight. Through scores of fights, Nightingale forgets her premonitions every time Bob lands safe. On the near thousandth flight, Nightingale hears that Bob's plane crashes. Nightingale concludes 'I knew he would crash', totally forgetting the hundreds of flights concerning which she felt the same unease. In fact your chances of dying in a commercial airline crash are more like ten million to one, but of course such crashes do happen, so that it is near inevitable that some Nightingale-like individual out there is going to have a dream of an air disaster a good portion of the time that such disasters do occur.

Related, more mundane paradoxes occur when we wait for buses, subway trains, or elevators. Suppose I take the crosstown subway train several stops to the west to go to work in the morning, returning eastward in the late afternoon. I notice that, in the morning, there are often one, two, even three trains going east before I finally get one that goes west. In the evening, on the other hand, I notice that there are often one, two or even three trains going west before I finally get my east-bound one. 'Damn it,' I conclude, 'they run more trains east in the morning, and more trains west in the evening.' The chap next to me comments, 'No, it is the other way around.' Living where I work and working where I live, he has had the mirror experience of mine. The mistake we both made was to fail to realise that when the train we want arrives, we get on it and so fail to notice that it may be followed by one or two more, going our way, before a train going the other way shows up.

Some twenty years ago physicist William Newcomb recently proposed a paradox that further illuminates the themes of this chapter.

A superbeing, Alpha, has demonstrated an ability to predict human behaviour, particularly when humans make choices between two bets about two boxes. Box A is open and clearly contains $1,000. Box B is closed and either contains $1,000,000 or nothing. Alpha offers humans two options: (1) pick the contents of A and B; (2) pick the contents of B. Alpha adds however that if he predicts that you will opt for 1, he will leave B empty, while if he predicts that you will opt for 2, he will leave $1,000,000 in B. Alpha has always been correct in his predictions about human choices (and he has not achieved this record through after-the-fact Fast-Eddie-fiddling with the boxes). He now offers you the choice between 1 and 2.

You might reason that since Alpha has been so accurate in his predictions, you surely ought to take option 2, and so gain $1,000,000. (There is something just a touch paradoxical about this 'choice' in that if Alpha confidently and correctly predicted you would make it, surely he must know something about your neurology or character that makes your action not a choice but an inevitability. If there isn't anything that affords a reliable prediction that you will opt for 2, if it is a real, unpredictable choice, then it may not do you any good to pick 2, because Alpha won't have predicted you would.)

You might, on the other hand, reason that box B already either has a million in it or it doesn't, and since your choice will not change this fact, you might as well take option 1 and collect the $1,000, along with whatever is in box B. In other words, option 1 gets you everything option 2 does, plus $1,000 dollars.

What may make option 2 attractive may be a belief in 'backward causation', a hunch that if I choose box B this will somehow cause Alpha to have put the million in the box, whereas if I choose both boxes, this will somehow cause Alpha to have taken the million out. This kind of wishful thinking is certainly common enough among humans, but there is no evidence that backward causation ever occurs or even could occur. If we exclude this kind of reasoning, it would seem that taking both boxes is the rational choice. However, I might reflect that perhaps Alpha likes wishful thinkers and he picks them out for his experiments knowing that they will pick box B. So he is rewarding wishful irrationality. But while you can, rationally, decide to pretend to be irrational, you can't rationally decide to be irrational, particularly retroactively. Knowing what Alpha was about you might take a course of drugs, or chants and meditations, to make yourself into the kind of person who would automatically reach for box B. *Then* you might hope he would make you the offer. But that doesn't help your choice right now. Moreover it is no sort of answer to the question, 'What is the rational choice?' to say, 'To have become irrational in a certain way long ago.'

R.M. Sainsbury has suggested that Newcomb's Paradox is closely related to the Prisoner's Dilemma, long a central conundrum of game theory, the mathematical theory of self-interested strategy in situations where choices must be made with incomplete information. Suppose we are both arrested for robbery. We are interrogated simultaneously and separately, the re-

sults, in years of jail time, of our independent decisions
to confess or not appear in the following table:

		YOU	
		confess	not confess
	confess	4\4	0\8
I			
	not confess	8\0	2\2

If both confess, we both get a sentence of four years; if
we both keep our mouths shut, we both spend two
years in jail. However, if I do not confess and you do,
I spend eight years in jail and you go free; the other
way round if you confess while I keep my mouth shut.
Given that I make my decision after (or independently
of) yours, I have to face the fact that you have confessed
or not confessed, and what I do cannot change that. If
you have confessed, my best move is to confess (if not,
I serve eight years rather than four); if you have not
confessed, my best move is to confess (if not, I serve
two years rather than none). So my best strategic
move, if you have confessed or if you have not confessed, is to confess. This same reasoning, of course,
makes you captive, too. Your best strategy must be
confession (you cannot change what I have done, your
decision can have no backward causality effect on that,

so you can only choose confession, which will be best for you whatever I have done).

The paradox of the Prisoner's Dilemma is that of course we would both do better if we both kept mum rather than confessing, but since what I can do will have no effect on your choice, my best rationally self-interested choice has to be to confess, for it is superior whichever choice you have made (and the reverse reasoning makes it clear you should confess). Over several decades game theorists have agreed that to confess is doleful rationality; if economics is the 'dismal science', the one-time Prisoner's Dilemma is its epitome. The Dilemma has become the name for any situation in which the payoff matrix is such that the two of us will do better if we cooperate (i.e. both not confess) than if we both defect, *but* either of us will do best if we defect while the other cooperates, and worst if we cooperate while the other defects. Stripped bare, you can see that almost all of our interactions with others have Prisoner's Dilemma aspects. When you buy almost anything, the seller may be concealing a defect, and you may be passing counterfeit money or a bad cheque; analogous features appear in our other interactions with people. If one has to interact with Fast Eddie, shouldn't one assume he will cheat/defect (and aside from all the Fast Eddies, won't there be lots of people just taking precautions against Fast Eddies)? As the mithridative poet put it,

> I'd face it as a wise man would,
> And train for ill and not for good.

As we will soon see, there is also wisdom in training

for good, or, even better, training to recognise which situations call for which mind set.

While game theorists have long agreed that rational self-interest requires one to defect in a one-shot Prisoner's Dilemma encounter, it has seemed less clear what is rational if one is going to play a series of games against the same opponent, or, more generally, several such series with different opponents. Again we find a case where we need to supplement our theorising with actual tests. In 1979 political scientist Robert Axelrod organised a tournament between computer programs for playing the Prisoner's Dilemma repeatedly against a number of opponents. The payoff matrix was put in positive terms. Players would score 1 point if both defected, 3 if both cooperated, and if one defected and the other cooperated the defector would get 5 points and the cooperator 0. The programs could store the results of each encounter with each of the other programs, so that it could adjust its strategy to differences in what the other programs did to it. Psychologists, economists, sociologists, mathematicians and political scientists from all over the world submitted fourteen programs. The results were quite unexpected.

The clear winner, in each of five tournaments, was TIT-FOR-TAT, submitted by Anatol Rapoport. Suggestively, it was the shortest program (the longest program did the worst): *obviousness* turned out to be a crucial ingredient of a winning strategy, *deviousness* was a fatal flaw. TIT-FOR-TAT's strategy was simplicity itself. It cooperated on its first encounter with any other program; hence it is called 'nice', as opposed to 'nasty', the label for programs that will sometimes defect without provocation. After the first encounter TIT-FOR-TAT would simply copy the previous move of its opponent; hence it was called 'provocable' *and* 'forgiving', since it punished defection but would return to cooperation as soon as the opponent 'paid up'. To reverse that trite cynical motto of American football and free enterprise, it appears, paradoxically, that *nice guys finish first.* To know TIT-FOR-TAT is to know that it cannot be beaten.

I hasten to add that this engaging result does not apply to what we most customarily call games, e.g. football, chess, poker, etc. For these *zero-sum games*, in which 'my loss is your gain' (and vice versa), there is no way for cooperation to evolve. In Prisoner's Dilemma interactions, mutual cooperation is more profitable than mutual defection, so cooperation can evolve (against the ever-present temptation to profit even more, through defection). Note the features that fire this evolution: the repeated interactions, the identifiability of other players, and clearness of the payoff results. To put it another way: don't buy a wrist watch from a man on a street corner whom you will never see again. It is possible that game theorists suffer from a tendency to see the world in the cut-throat zero-sum terms appropriate to literal games (in which we tolerate the zero-sum structure because 'it's just a game', because the result is momentary and, except in professional sports, of little importance). The fourteen submitted programs contained many nasty programs and these did very badly.

Perhaps it is not just game theorists that tend to see things in zero-sum terms. Axelrod set some students, who hadn't studied game theory, to playing the same game that the computer programs had played. Though told to maximise their individual score and not to worry if the other players also did well, the human players tended to adopt self-destructive nasty strategies.

(To inject a personal experience, my wife and I were invited to dinner by a Japanese family in Miyazaki, Kyushu. Their six-year-old daughter, and eight- and nine-year-old sons, were delightfully outspoken parties to the dinner, in which we all rolled sushi together and ate it up. At the end of the meal one of the boys insisted that we play cards and asked me to teach them to play an American card game. I started us off playing one of the many games in which the winner is the one who first manages to discard all of his or her cards. After someone had done this one of the boys immediately demanded, 'Now, how do we tell the second winner?' I immediately invented additional rules so that, after more play, there would indeed be a 'second winner'. I did not need prompting to invent the additional rules which would produce a third, fourth, fifth and sixth winner. I felt that I had been taught rather more than I had taught.)

TIT-FOR-TAT is not an absolutely infallible strategy. It goes wrong, for example, in the land of the nasties, where everyone always defects. Though, interestingly, if there are more than 5 per cent TIT-FOR-TATers in the land of the nasties, TIT-FOR-TAT becomes a viable strategy. This gives a kind of answer to the biblical question as to how many just men a city must contain to make it worth preserving.

After the first set of tournaments, Axelrod circulated the results and called for improved programs for another tournament. Naturally, among the much larger number of programs submitted, few nasty programs appeared. TIT-FOR-TAT again proved a winner, though not by as salient a margin. There were only two interesting competitors, possible candidates for a slight superiority. One was TWO-TITS-FOR-A-TAT; it would not provoke until the opposing program defected twice. Another program, otherwise identical to TIT-FOR-TAT, would occasionally try switching to cooperate, if it were locked into a long series of defect/defect plays (shades of nasty land), all in hopes of jarring the other program back into cooperative mode.

TIT-FOR-TAT, the eponym for the evolution of cooperation, is a most engaging *meme*, one which casts light on a startling range of features of our world. On the static fronts in northern France during World War I, where the same troops shelled each other for months at a time, a pattern informally and unspokenly evolved in which both sides would cease fire for an hour or so each day (during which time the soldiers on both sides would do all the many things one can't do when protectively entrenched under sand and concrete, only to return hurriedly underground when the understood safe period was over). The general staff would periodically introduce cooperation-dispelling shakeups by rotating divisions or their officers or by sending in corrective officers, but the same unspoken cooperation would reappear after a time. More mundanely, the TIT-FOR-TAT *meme* explains why you need the cushion of inspectors and realtors when you buy or sell a house, while neither you nor your neighbourhood grocer needs this precaution in your repeated interactions. Similarly, people don't lock their doors in many isolated small towns, while a plethora of locks, alarms and metal doors characterise city life.

TIT-FOR-TAT is a strategy that wants itself known. Its success depends on the assumption of predictability, automaticity, even irrational habituation, not choice at all. Indeed the model works to explain completely mindless biological activity, down to the bacterial level. Axelrod and biologist William Hamilton write that

> ALL D[efect] is the primeval stage and is evolutionarily stable. But cooperation based on reciprocity can gain a foothold through two different mechanisms. First, there can be kinship between mutant strategies, giving the genes of the mutants some stake in each other's success, thereby altering the payoff of the interaction when viewed from the perspective of the gene rather than the individual. A second mechanism to overcome total defection is for the mutant strategies to arrive in a cluster so that they provide a nontrivial proportion of the interactions each has... Once a variety of strategies is present, TIT-FOR-TAT is an extremely robust one. It does well in a wide range of circumstances and gradually displaces all other strategies in an ecological simulation that contains a great variety of more or less sophisticated decision rules.
>
> R. Axelrod, *The Evolution of Cooperation*, p. 99

Axelrod and Hamilton provide us with a much more specific, and charmingly bizarre, instance (p. 98).

> A species of sea bass have the sexual organs of both the male and the female. They form pairs and roughly may be said to take turns at being the high investment partner (laying eggs) and low investment partner (providing sperm to fertilise eggs). Up to ten spawnings occur in a day and only

a few eggs are provided each time. Pairs tend to break up if sex roles are not divided evenly.

Successful explanation over a wide range of biological phenomena suggests the hand of nature, which is to say the selfish genes. Have we discovered a deeply pervasive facet of nature or have we (Rapoport, Axelrod, et al.) created a particularly penetrating *meme*, an intellectual replicator, like the Liar, that is rapidly spreading through our cognitive world? The answer to this either/or question is of course a fecundly paradoxical 'Yes'.

Do you read me?

Some Other Paradoxes

Achilles and the Tortoise

Zeno, a fifth-century BC Greek philosopher who lived in Elea, authored a number of paradoxes about infinite series, the best known of which concerns a footrace. To give the now traditional version, we imagine Achilles, the swiftest of Greek warriors, racing against a tortoise, which is, naturally, given a head start. When Achilles begins, the tortoise is, say, 100 feet ahead; after Achilles has covered 100 feet the tortoise is 10 feet ahead; after Achiless has covered that 10 feet the tortoise is still 1 foot ahead; since the series 1/10, 1/100, 1/1000, 1/10,000, etc. has no termination, the tortoise will always be a little bit ahead of Achilles.

This is Zeno's *second* argument against our ordinary notions of motion, time and space. The first, the Race Track, argues that to cover the track, one has to cover half of it; to cover half, a quarter; to cover a quarter, an eighth; to cover an eighth, a sixteenth; and so on, indefinitely. The third, the Arrow, makes related points about the flight of an arrow; the fourth, the Stadium, about movements of files of troops on a field. As Borges acutely observes, there is no evidence that Zeno himself personified his racers as Achilles or, still less, a tortoise (*Labyrinths*, p. 203). Achilles first appears as Aristotle's name for the paradox, and the tortoise seeps in much later in the A-Z loops. Borges comments, 'I would like to know the name of the poet who provided it with a hero and a tortoise.' Shades of Borges's Tlön, however, we may well suspect that it was the energy of *meme* itself that added them. Interestingly, the Chinese philosopher Hui Tzu independently authored Zenoesque paradoxes in the fourth century BC. (The acute reader may have noticed that I have done some A-Z loop work, simplifying and neatening up originals. Strictly speaking, the 'All Cretans' Liar paradox is only paradoxical when tightened to 'I am now lying'. Barry's original formulation of his paradox made use of syllables rather than words; Grelling used 'autological' to mean *self-descriptive* and 'heterological' to mean *non-self-descriptive*.)

The Heap and the Bald Man

These puzzles of Eubulides of Miletus are today often termed problems about vagueness rather than paradoxes. Imagine a heap of pea gravel. Removing a single stone doesn't change it from being a heap to not being a heap. So remove another, and another, and another; though removing a stone can't change it from a heap to a non-heap, eventually we will have nothing left, which, while perhaps a heap of nothing, is not a heap. Similarly, removing a single hair surely cannot change someone from hairy to bald, but if we keep on pulling one after another...

Some Other Paradoxes

The Lawyer

Protagoras, a fifth-century teacher of rhetoric, was supposed to have contracted with his students that each was to pay him tuition if and only if they won their first case. One of his students, Euathlus, sued him for free tuition, arguing that 'If I win the case, then I win free tuition, as that is what I am suing for; if I lose, then my tuition is free, since this is my first case.' Protagoras, in court, is supposed to have responded, 'If you give judgement for Euathlus, then he will owe me a fee, since it is his first case and that was our agreement; if you give judgement for me, then he will owe me a fee, since that is the content of your judgement.'

The Surprise Execution

Also called the Hangman, the Sneak Quiz, etc. On Saturday the warden tells the prisoner that he will be executed at noon some day during the following week and the execution will be a surprise. The prisoner reasons that after next Friday's noon, the only remaining time for his execution will be Saturday noon, so the execution will be no surprise. Therefore, he reasons, he cannot be executed on Saturday, because of the lack of surprise. Consequently, however, as soon as Thursday noon passes, he can only be executed on Friday, because Saturday is ruled out; but, then, the Friday execution will be no surprise and hence a Friday execution is ruled out. If Saturday and Friday are ruled out, however, then when Wednesday noon has passed, Thursday will have to be the execution date.

But if Thursday has to be the execution date, then it will be no surprise, so it has to be ruled out. Given that Thursday is out, a Wednesday execution will come as no surprise; so we are back to Tuesday and, by similar reasoning, it is out, as is Monday and hence Sunday. So there can be no execution.

Hempel's Paradox

Each time we observe a black raven, we add to the confirmation of the claim that 'All ravens are black'. If we have just checked a few ravens, we have *weakly confirmed* that claim; if we have observed hundreds, we have *strongly confirmed* the claim; if we were able to observe all ravens, we could be said to have *conclusively confirmed* the claim that they are all black. 'All ravens are black' is logically equivalent to 'All non-black objects are not ravens'. So what if we observe a purple cow or a pink elephant? Do not these observations weakly confirm that 'All non-black objects are not ravens'? Hence, surely, these observations – of purple cows and pink elephants – confirm that 'All ravens are black'. Indeed, if you think about it, it would seem that we are constantly confirming that 'All ravens are black'.

Goodman's Grue Paradox

Philosopher Nelson Goodman invented a term, 'grue', which means 'green before 2000 AD and blue thereafter'. Consider all the observations that confirm that 'All emeralds are green'; since all of these observations were made before 2000 AD, all of these observations equally confirm that 'All emeralds are grue'! But how can it be that the bizarre speculation that 'All emeralds are grue' could have the same well-established status as the familiar fact that 'All emeralds are green'?

Elevator Paradoxes

Mr Grandman, whose palatial office comprises much of the twelfth floor of the fifteen-floor office building, has as usual seen two or three elevator cars going up before, finally, he gets one going down. 'Hah!' he exclaims, 'they must be flying the elevators off the roof to get rid of them.' On the second of the four subground floors, Maintenance Engineer Loman resignedly watches two down elevators go by before he gets an up one. 'They must be storing them in the lowest basement.' The explanation, however, removes Grandman and Loman's puzzlement. If there are, say, two elevators, the chances are that both will be *above* the second basement and *below* the twelfth floor, so it is likely that the two cars will reach the second basement *going down* before any car will come going up. Similarly, it is likely that two cars will reach the twelfth floor *going up* before any car will come going down. If you are on one of the middle floors, of course, it is as likely that you will get an up as a down at your first opportunity. Startlingly, the whole paradoxical effect disappears if the number of elevators reaches over twenty.

Sources and Suggested Reading

Axelrod, R. *The Evolution of Cooperation* (New York: Basic Books, 1985). A readable and influential explication of work on the iterated Prisoner's Dilemma with far-ranging applications.

Borges, J. *Labyrinths* (New York: New Directions, 1969). Contains a number of profound, brilliant and paradoxical narratives that are simultaneously first-rate philosophy and literature.

Brook, S., ed. *The Oxford Book of Dreams* (Oxford: Oxford University Press, 1983).

Buttrick, G. et al., eds. *The Interpreter's Bible* (New York: Abingdon Press, 1952).

Campbell, R. and Sowden, L., eds. *Paradoxes of Rationality and Cooperation: Prisoner's Dilemma and Newcomb's Problem* (Vancouver: University of British Columbia Press, 1985).

Carroll, L. *The Annotated Alice: Alice's Adventures in Wonderland and Through the Looking Glass*, ed. M. Gardner (New York: Clarkson N. Potter, Bramhall House, 1960).

Colie, R. *Paradoxica Epidemica: The Renaissance Tradition of Paradox* (Princeton: Princeton University Press, 1966). A scholarly and fascinating survey of the dominant role of paradox in fifteenth- and sixteenth-century European thought and literature.

Davis, M. *The Undecidable* (New York: Raven Press,

1965). Reproduces the original papers by K. Gödel and A. Turing that establish the incompleteness and undecidability of arithmetic. Heavy going.

Dawkins, R. *The Selfish Gene* (Oxford: Oxford University Press, 1976).

Dennett, D. *Consciousness Explained* (Boston: Little, Brown, 1991). A trenchant, profound and amusing examination of the paradoxes of consciousness, perception and cognition.

Gardner, M. *Aha! Gotcha: Paradoxes to Puzzle and Delight* (New York: W.H. Freeman). A truly delightful survey of paradoxes concerning logic, number, geometry, probability, statistics and time.

Goodman, N. *Fact, Fiction, and Forecast* (Cambridge, MA: Harvard University Press; 2nd ed., Indianapolis: Bobbs-Merrill, 1965).

Hofstadter, D. *Gödel, Escher, Bach: The Eternal Golden Braid* (New York: Random House, 1980). A brilliant and engaging presentation of the paradoxical results of Russell, Gödel and Turing, threaded through with insights into representation, thought, mechanism, mind, art and literature.

Hofstadter, D. *Metamagical Themas* (Basic Books, 1986). More, in short essay form, on a variety of puzzles and paradoxes, including the iterated Prisoner's Dilemma, Newcomb's Paradox, and many others.

Hofstadter, D. and Dennett, D. *The Mind's I: Fantasies and Reflections on the Self and Soul* (New York: Basic Books, 1981). A dazzling collection of essays and narratives by a variety of authors.

Huff, D. *How to Lie with Statistics* (New York: Norton, 1954). A wonderfully clear and readable how-to-do-it book.

Hughes, P. and Brecht, G. *Vicious Circles and Infinity: A Panoply of Paradoxes* (Garden City, New York: Doubleday, 1975). A delicious and spritely offering of scores of paradoxes.

Jennings, K. *The Devouring Fungus* (New York: W.W. Norton, 1990).

Kneale, W. and Kneale, M. *The Development of Logic* (Oxford: Oxford University Press, 1962). A scholarly but readable history of logic that includes a history of logical and mathematical paradoxes.

Leiber, J. *An Invitation to Cognitive Science* (Oxford: Basil Blackwell, 1991).

Leiber, J. *Can Animals and Machines Be Persons?* (Indianapolis: Hackett, 1985).

Liu, J. *Language – Paradox – Poetics* (Princeton: Princeton University Press, 1989). A brief and lucid attempt to trace the central place of paradox in Chinese literature with a powerful grasp of parallels in recent Western literary theory.

Russell, B. *Principia Mathematica* (Cambridge: Cambridge University Press, 1910-13).

Ryle, G. *Dilemmas* (Cambridge: Cambridge University Press, 1961). The title of this delightfully readable set of lectures could as appropriately have been 'Paradoxes'.

Sainsbury, R. *Paradoxes* (Cambridge: Cambridge University Press, 1988). A compact scholarly treatment of several central paradoxes.

Salmon, W. *Zeno's Paradoxes* (Indianapolis: Bobbs-Merrill, 1970). A collection of essays, some popular, some scholarly and some mathematically demanding. Professor Salmon provides a helpful and delightful introduction and appendix for the general reader.

Smullyan, R. *What Is the Name of This Book?* (Englewood Cliffs, New Jersey: Prentice-Hall, 1978). An amusing, free-wheeling and original tour of paradoxes.

Index

87

also available in the Interpretations series

FACTS

Bede Rundle

Fellow of Trinity College, Oxford

Facts have many contrasts: with fiction and fantasy, with speculation and opinion, with hypothesis and theory. Two contrasts of particular interest – to philosophy, to morality, to the natural and social sciences – are those of fact with theory and fact with value, and a central concern of this book is to examine arguments which would have us enlarge these domains at the expense of the realm of facts.

It is naturally supposed either that facts enjoy a concrete existence, being numbered among such worldly items as events, or that they possess a more abstract character, having their home in language. Both alternatives are the source of difficulties, encouraging sceptical claims that the existence of facts is unknowable and their nature impenetrable. An analysis of *fact* is offered which, in rejecting both possibilities, seeks to remove the mystery which surrounds this key concept.

ISBN 0 7156 2467 9

also available in the Interpretations series

LAWS OF NATURE

Rom Harré

Fellow of Linacre College, Oxford

The laws of nature, on which all science is based, are supposed to have three characteristics: to be supported by evidence, to be universally applicable, and to enable us to predict what will always happen in the same circumstances. In this book a philosopher of science examines some of the well-known laws of nature from the point of view of all three characteristics. He shows that science is possible only within a metaphysical framework, a general assumption of the existence of natural kinds. The idea is used to explicate the scope and modality of laws of nature and also to resolve some of the classical paradoxes which have emerged when they are studied in the light of their logical form alone.

ISBN 0 7156 2464 4

also available from Duckworth

MIND MATTERS

Series editor: Judith Hughes

Many philosophy books claim to be written for the general reader as well as the academic, but all too few really cater for their needs. This series explores philosophical issues and is written specifically for the general reader.

Each book starts with the kind of question we may ask ourselves without, perhaps, realising that we are 'philosophising'. Do computers have minds? Can a pile of bricks be a work of art? Should we hold pathological killers responsible for their crimes? These questions are explored and new questions raised with frequent reference to the views of the major philosophers.

The books in the 'Mind Matters' series are concise, lively, inexpensive, jargon-free and, above all, a fascinating read.

ART OR BUNK?
Ian Ground

For many people, the infamous pile of bricks in the Tate Gallery, Carl André's *Equivalent VIII*, is still the most potent symbol of modern art, and it is what inspires Ian Ground's question 'Art or Bunk?' Using his wide knowledge of classical aesthetics and current ideas in the philosophy of art, he guides us through various attempts to say just what sort of thing a work of art is, and shows us a way to answer the question. Although his examples relate to the visual arts, his arguments are applicable to arts in general, and his book provides a much-needed lively and readable introduction to aesthetics.

Hbk ISBN 1-85399-014-0 £17.95
Pbk ISBN 1-85399-015-9 £6.95

BEFORE EUREKA
the presocratics and their science
Robin Waterfield

What kind of science and scientific thinking went on in the West before the familiar names of Aristotle and Archimedes claimed centre stage? Actually an extraordinary amount – extraordinary both in volume and in breadth of scale. Their enterprise was no less than to describe and explain the whole universe and all its major constituent parts. Their achievement was to establish the authenticity of the rational human mind as a tool for tackling the universe in a matter-of-fact manner.

Robin Waterfield not only describes the Presocratic enterprise in a clear and lively way, he also questions what science is, and whether the Presocratics were scientists in the modern sense of the word. As his previous publications range from the sublimity of Greek philosophy to the fantasy of children's space-age fiction, he is well qualified to write this book.

Hbk ISBN 1-85399-074-4 £17.95
Pbk ISBN 1-85399-075-2 £6.95

CAN'T WE MAKE MORAL JUDGEMENTS?
Mary Midgley

How many times do we hear the statement, 'It's not for me to judge'? It conveys one of the most popular ideas of our time: that to make judgements of others is essentially wrong. But doesn't this idea itself involve a moral judgement? What is it? Could we possibly avoid making it? Why have so many thinkers urged us to do this impossible thing?

In this lively and approachable discussion, Mary Midgley turns a spotlight on the fashionable view that we no longer need or use moral judgements. Guiding the reader through the diverse approaches to the complex subject, she points out the strong confident beliefs about such things as the value of freedom that underlie our supposed scepticism about values. She shows how the question of whether or not we can make moral judgements must inevitably affect our attitudes not only to the law and its institutions, but also to events that occur in our daily lives, and suggests that mistrust of moral judgement may be making life even harder for us than it would be otherwise.

Pbk ISBN 1-85399-166-X   £6.95

DOES GOD EXIST?
Mark Corner

Do people talking about God know what they are talking about? Are they all talking about the same thing? How do different religions approach the existence of God? Can God's existence be proved? And even if it can, is God necessarily good?

Does God Exist? sets out to provide a lively and readable introduction to the main issues of theism and atheism. The author takes a fresh look at the question that has always been at the very roots of philosophy. His arguments provoke further interest as a source of new ideas.

Pbk ISBN 1-85399-164-3 £6.95

DO WE HAVE FREE WILL?
Mark Thornton

'Do We Have Free Will?' is not just an abstract philosophical question. It shapes educational and legal theory, it underlies particular views in Sociology and Psychology, and it is apparent in decisions in social and political policy.

Mark Thornton has produced a comprehensive guide to the rich variety of philosophical opinion on the subject. His clear exposition, penetrating criticism and original suggestions make this a valuable book for anyone with a practical or theoretical concern with issues of human freedom and responsibility.

Hbk ISBN 1-85399-018-3 £17.95
Pbk ISBN 1-85399-019-1 £6.95

2077

MAD OR BAD?
Michael Bavidge

Michael Bavidge's question, 'Mad or Bad?' arises out of a long-standing philosophical interest in the connections between ethics and the philosophy of mind and from surprise at the verdicts in some notorious murder trials. Dreadful crimes demand total, unreserved condemnation and heavy punishment, but their very dreadfulness also leads us to think, 'Anyone who does *that* must be mad!'

This book provides a thought-provoking and sensitive new attempt to show us how we can preserve our ordinary moral intuitions about dreadful crimes while facing up to the difficulties of holding psychopathic criminals fully responsible for their actions. It is an important topic with wide-ranging implications which affect us all.

Hbk ISBN 1-85399-016-7 £17.95
Pbk ISBN 1-85399-017-5 £6.95

MINDS, BRAINS AND MACHINES
Geoffrey Brown

Whether or not machines can think is the stuff of which dreams and nightmares are made. Geoffrey Brown lives in this world, however, and his expertise in computer engineering gives him a down-to-earth view of the present complexity and future possibilities of the machines which appear to control much of our lives.

But he is also a philosopher who sees that the question demands careful consideration of some fundamental issues. What do we mean by 'think'? Is machine 'thinking' like human 'thinking'? What does it mean to be conscious? And in answering these questions we reach the heart of what is called the philosophy of mind.

Hbk ISBN 1-85399-012-4 £17.95
Pbk ISBN 1-85399-013-2 £6.95

REASONABLE CARE
Grant Gillett

If any discipline poses questions of life and death it is medical ethics. Where the availability of treatment is limited, who should get priority? Should doctors force treatment on unwilling patients? How can we judge whether a life is worth living and who should decide? *Reasonable Care* helps us approach these questions by offering a survey and critique of contemporary medical ethics, but it does so by drawing heavily on actual practice and the problems faced by doctors, nurses and their patients.

Grant Gillett is ideally placed to straddle the philosophical and the practical worlds, because when he is not writing and teaching philosophy he spends his time doing neurosurgery.

Hbk ISBN 1-85399-072-8 £17.95
Pbk ISBN 1-85399-073-6 £6.95